MANGA SHAKESPEARE

HENRI

ADAPTED BY
RICHARD APPIGNANESI

ILLUSTRATED BY
PATRICK WARREN

SELF MADE HERO

In association with
Historic Royal PALACES

In association with
Historic Royal
PALACES

This is a special collaboration between SelfMadeHero and Historic
Royal Palaces. Hampton Court Palace is one of the great survivals
from the era of Henry VIII, and special celebrations of Henry VIII's
reign begin there in 2009. Patrick Warren, the artist, visited
Hampton Court Palace to help his research for creating the
backgrounds in the book. As well as sketching the palace interiors
and exteriors, he used archive material to re-create the costumes
and environment of Tudor England.

Published by
SelfMadeHero
A division of Metro Media Ltd
5 Upper Wimpole Street
London W1G 6BP
www.selfmadehero.com

This edition published 2009

Illustrator: Patrick Warren
Text Adaptor: Richard Appignanesi
Designer: Andy Huckle
Toner: Ryuta Osada
Textual Consultant: Nick de Somogyi
Publishing Director: Emma Hayley
With thanks to: David Souden, Sarah Kilby, Kent Rawlinson,
Claire Murphy and Doug Wallace

ISBN: 978-1-906838-02-7

10 9 8 7 6 5 4 3 2 1
Printed and bound in Slovenia

Henry VIII, King of England

"You have half our power!"

Anne Boleyn, Henry's second Queen

*"By my troth,
I would not
be a Queen!"*

*"Truth loves
open dealing!"*

Katherine of Aragon, Henry's first Queen

Cardinal Campeius of Rome, legate of the Pope

"To your highness' hand I tender my commission..."

Cardinal Thomas Wolsey, Archbishop of York

"I have ventured far beyond my depth..."

"The good I stand on is my truth and honesty!"

Thomas Cranmer, Archbishop of Canterbury

"That's the plain truth!"

Stephen Gardiner, the King's secretary, later Bishop of Winchester

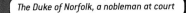

The Duke of Norfolk, a nobleman at court

"*This is the Cardinal's doing...*"

Lord Abergavenny, son-in-law to Buckingham

The Duke of Buckingham, a nobleman at court

"*The net has fallen upon me!*"

"*I do know kinsmen that have sickened their estates!*"

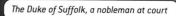

Lord Chamberlain, adviser to the King

The Duke of Suffolk, a nobleman at court

"The King,
the King!"

"O,
'tis true!"

Thomas Cromwell, secretary to Cardinal Wolsey

"Men so noble should
find respect!"

Thomas Lovell, Marshal of the House
Lord Sands, a nobleman at court
"The red wine must rise in their cheeks!"
"That churchman bears a bounteous mind indeed!"
"Will this work?"
The Earl of Surrey, son-in-law to Buckingham

Two Gentlemen of the court
“Is he found guilty?’
“Yes, truly he is!”
An Old Lady of the court
A Surveyor to the Duke of Buckingham
“Eminence, wealth, sovereignty are blessings. . .”
“On my soul, I’ll speak but truth!”

THE SIX WIVES OF KING HENRY VIII

Henry VIII
(1491–1547)

Katherine of Aragon
(1485–1536)

married Arthur, Prince of Wales:
November 1501
widowed: April 1502
married Henry VIII:
June 1509
divorced: May 1533
[Divorce proceedings 1527–1533]

daughter: Mary I
(born February 1516)

Anne Boleyn
(c.1500–1536)

married Henry VIII:
January 1533
executed for adultery:
May 1536

daughter: Elizabeth I
(born September 1533)

Jane Seymour
(1509–1537)

married Henry VIII:
May 1536
died: October 1537

son: Edward VI
(born October 1537)

Anne of Cleves
(1515–1557)

married Henry VIII:
January 1540
divorced:
July 1540

Catherine Howard
(c.1522–1542)

married Henry VIII:
July 1540
executed for adultery:
February 1542

Kateryn Parr
(1512–1548)

married Henry VIII:
July 1543

THE FRENCH ALL IN GOLD, LIKE HEATHEN GODS, SHONE DOWN THE ENGLISH AND MADE BRITAIN, INDIA.

THE MADAMS TOO, NOT USED TO TOIL, DID ALMOST SWEAT TO BEAR THE PRIDE UPON THEM.

THEIR VERY LABOUR WAS TO THEM AS A PAINTING.

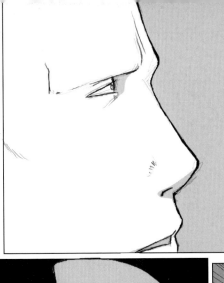

WHO SET THE BODY AND THE LIMBS OF THIS GREAT SPORT TOGETHER?

THE DEVIL SPEED HIM! NO MAN'S PIE IS FREED FROM HIS AMBITIOUS FINGER.

ALL THIS WAS ORDERED BY THE CARDINAL OF YORK.

I WONDER THAT SUCH A KEECH CAN WITH HIS VERY BULK TAKE UP THE RAYS OF THE BENEFICIAL SUN AND KEEP IT FROM THE EARTH.

NOT PROPPED BY ANCESTRY, NOR CALLED UPON FOR HIGH FEATS DONE TO THE CROWN...

BUT SPIDER-LIKE, OUT OF HIS SELF-DRAWING WEB, OF HIS OWN MERIT MAKES HIS WAY, WHICH BUYS A PLACE NEXT TO THE KING.

WHY THE DEVIL TOOK HE UPON HIM, WITHOUT THE PRIVITY OF THE KING, TO APPOINT WHO SHOULD ATTEND ON HIM? ALL THE GENTRY — TO WHOM AS GREAT A CHARGE AS LITTLE HONOUR HE MEANT TO LAY UPON.

WHENCE HAS HE THAT, IF NOT FROM HELL?

CARDINAL THOMAS WOLSEY, WITH HIS SECRETARY AND GUARDS, PASSES BY.

LO, WHERE COMES THAT ROCK THAT I ADVISE YOUR SHUNNING.

THIS BUTCHER'S CUR IS GONE TO THE KING — I'LL FOLLOW AND OUTSTARE HIM.

STAY, MY LORD, AND LET YOUR REASON QUESTION WHAT 'TIS YOU GO ABOUT.

I'LL TO THE KING AND CRY DOWN THIS FELLOW'S INSOLENCE.

BE ADVISED, HEAT NOT A FURNACE FOR YOUR FOE SO HOT THAT IT DO SINGE YOURSELF.

SIR, I AM THANKFUL TO YOU...

BUT THIS TOP-PROUD FELLOW I DO KNOW TO BE CORRUPT AND TREASONOUS.

SAY NOT "TREASONOUS".

TO THE KING I'LL SAY IT. THIS HOLY FOX, ONLY TO SHOW HIS POMP AS WELL IN FRANCE AS HERE AT HOME, SUGGESTS THE KING TO THIS LAST COSTLY TREATY THAT SWALLOWED SO MUCH TREASURE.

BRANDON, A SERGEANT-AT-ARMS, APPROACHES WITH A DETACHMENT OF ARMED GUARDS.

TMM!

MY LORD DUKE OF BUCKINGHAM, I ARREST THEE OF HIGH TREASON, IN THE NAME OF OUR MOST SOVEREIGN KING.

THE NET HAS FALLEN UPON ME! I SHALL PERISH.

I AM SORRY: 'TIS HIS HIGHNESS' PLEASURE YOU SHALL TO THE TOWER.

IT WILL HELP ME NOTHING TO PLEAD MINE INNOCENCE FOR THAT DYE IS ON ME WHICH MAKES MY WHITEST PART BLACK.

HERE IS A WARRANT FROM THE KING TO ATTACH LORD MONTAGUE, THE DUKE'S CONFESSOR JOHN COURT, ONE GILBERT PARK, HIS CHANCELLOR —

NO MORE, I HOPE.

A MONK OF THE CHARTREUX.

NICHOLAS HOPKINS?

HE!

MY SURVEYOR IS FALSE. THE CARDINAL HATH SHOWED HIM GOLD.

MY LIFE IS SPANNED ALREADY. I AM THE SHADOW OF POOR BUCKINGHAM.

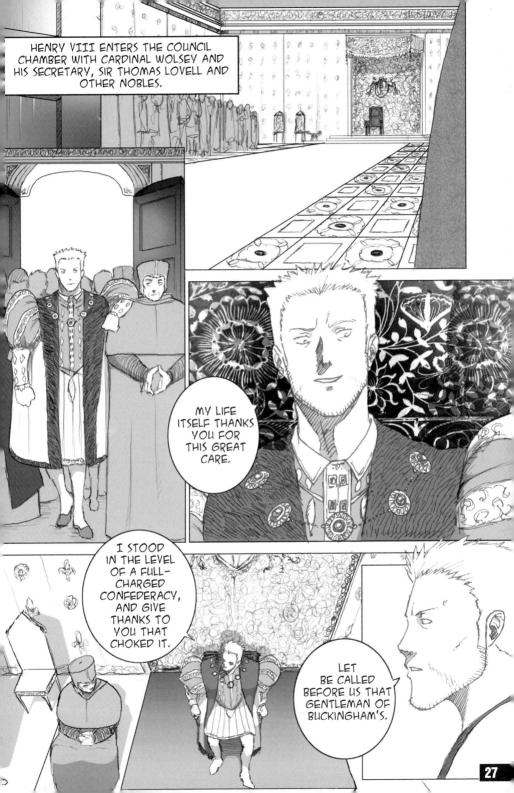

HENRY VIII ENTERS THE COUNCIL CHAMBER WITH CARDINAL WOLSEY AND HIS SECRETARY, SIR THOMAS LOVELL AND OTHER NOBLES.

MY LIFE ITSELF THANKS YOU FOR THIS GREAT CARE.

I STOOD IN THE LEVEL OF A FULL-CHARGED CONFEDERACY, AND GIVE THANKS TO YOU THAT CHOKED IT.

LET BE CALLED BEFORE US THAT GENTLEMAN OF BUCKINGHAM'S.

QUEEN KATHERINE ENTERS WITH THE DUKES OF NORFOLK AND SUFFOLK.

I'LL HEAR HIS CONFESSIONS.

ARISE AND TAKE PLACE BY US. YOU HAVE HALF OUR POWER.

PECK

MAJESTY, YOUR HONOUR IS THE POINT OF MY PETITION.

LADY MINE, PROCEED.

LORD CARDINAL, THEY VENT REPROACHES MOST BITTERLY ON YOU, AS PUTTER-ON OF THESE EXACTIONS.

THE KING OUR MASTER — EVEN HE ESCAPES NOT LANGUAGE UNMANNERLY WHICH ALMOST APPEARS IN LOUD REBELLION.

YOUR SUBJECTS ARE IN GREAT GRIEVANCE. THERE HAVE BEEN COMMISSIONS SENT DOWN AMONG 'EM WHICH HATH FLAWED THE HEART OF ALL THEIR LOYALTIES.

NOT "ALMOST APPEARS", IT *DOTH* APPEAR!

FOR, UPON THESE TAXATIONS, THE CLOTHIERS HAVE PUT OFF THE SPINSTERS, CARDERS, WEAVERS, WHO, COMPELLED BY HUNGER, ARE ALL IN UPROAR.

WHAT TAXATION? MY LORD CARDINAL, YOU THAT ARE BLAMED FOR IT ALIKE WITH US, KNOW YOU OF THIS TAXATION?

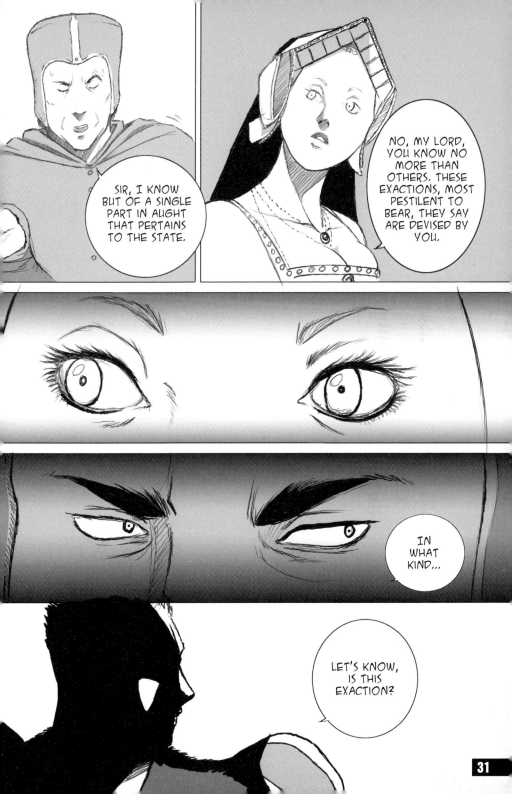

IF I AM TRADUCED BY IGNORANT TONGUES, LET ME SAY 'TIS BUT THE FATE THAT VIRTUE MUST GO THROUGH.

WE MUST NOT STINT OUR NECESSARY ACTIONS IN THE FEAR TO COPE MALICIOUS CENSURERS. IN FEAR, WE SHOULD TAKE ROOT OR SIT STATE-STATUES ONLY.

THINGS DONE WELL EXEMPT THEMSELVES FROM FEAR...

SIXTH PART OF EACH?

WHY, WE TAKE FROM EVERY TREE LOP, BARK AND PART OF THE TIMBER!

TO EVERY COUNTY SEND OUR LETTERS WITH FREE PARDON TO EACH MAN THAT HAS DENIED THE FORCE OF THIS COMMISSION. PRAY, LOOK TO IT.

A WORD WITH YOU.

NOD

LET IT BE NOISED THAT THROUGH OUR INTERCESSION THIS REVOKEMENT AND PARDON COMES.

I AM SORRY THAT THE DUKE OF BUCKINGHAM IS RUN IN YOUR DISPLEASURE.

IT GRIEVES MANY. SIT BY US, YOU SHALL HEAR OF HIM THINGS TO STRIKE HONOUR SAD.

THE DUKE OF BUCKINGHAM'S SURVEYOR.

WITH BOLD SPIRIT RELATE WHAT YOU HAVE COLLECTED OUT OF THE DUKE OF BUCKINGHAM.

SPEAK FREELY.

EVERY DAY IT WOULD INFECT HIS SPEECH, THAT IF THE KING SHOULD WITHOUT ISSUE DIE, HE'LL CARRY IT SO TO MAKE THE SCEPTRE HIS. THESE VERY WORDS I'VE HEARD HIM UTTER TO HIS SON-IN-LAW, LORD ABERGAVENNY, TO WHOM BY OATH HE MENACED REVENGE UPON THE CARDINAL.

HOW GROUNDED HE HIS TITLE TO THE CROWN?

HE WAS BROUGHT TO THIS BY A VAIN PROPHECY OF NICHOLAS HOPKINS.

WHAT WAS THAT HOPKINS?

SIR, A CHARTREUX FRIAR, HIS CONFESSOR, WHO FED HIM WORDS OF SOVEREIGNTY.

HOW KNOW'ST THOU THIS?

NOT LONG BEFORE YOUR HIGHNESS SPED TO FRANCE, THE DUKE DID OF ME DEMAND WHAT WAS THE SPEECH AMONG THE LONDONERS CONCERNING THE FRENCH JOURNEY...

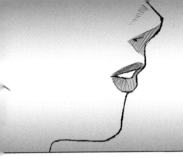

TAKE HEED YOU CHARGE NOT A NOBLE PERSON.

ON MY SOUL, I'LL SPEAK BUT TRUTH. I TOLD THE DUKE, BY THE DEVIL'S ILLUSIONS THE MONK MIGHT BE DECEIVED AND DANGEROUS.

HE ANSWERED, "TUSH, IT CAN DO ME NO DAMAGE,"

ADDING THAT, HAD THE KING IN HIS LAST SICKNESS FAILED, THE CARDINAL'S AND SIR THOMAS LOVELL'S HEADS SHOULD HAVE GONE OFF.

AH HA! THERE'S MISCHIEF IN THIS MAN.

CANST THOU SAY FURTHER?

GOD MEND ALL!

NOW, MADAM, MAY HIS HIGHNESS LIVE IN FREEDOM, AND THIS MAN OUT OF PRISON?

THERE'S SOMETHING MORE — WHAT SAY'ST?

THE LORD CHAMBERLAIN AND LORD SANDS DISCUSS RECENT EVENTS.

IS IT POSSIBLE THE SPELLS OF FRANCE SHOULD JUGGLE MEN INTO SUCH STRANGE MYSTERIES?

NEW CUSTOMS, THOUGH NEVER SO RIDICULOUS, YET ARE FOLLOWED.

WHAT NEWS, SIR THOMAS LOVELL?

I HEAR OF NONE BUT THE NEW PROCLAMATION THAT'S CLAPPED UPON THE COURT-GATE.

WHAT IS IT FOR?

THE REFORMATION OF OUR TRAVELLED GALLANTS THAT FILL THE COURT WITH QUARRELS...

THEY MUST LEAVE THOSE REMNANTS OF FOOL AND FEATHER THAT THEY GOT IN FRANCE, RENOUNCING CLEAN THE FAITH THEY HAVE IN TENNIS, TALL STOCKINGS, AND SHORT BREECHES, AND UNDERSTAND AGAIN LIKE HONEST MEN.

THEIR DISEASES ARE GROWN CATCHING. I AM GLAD THEY ARE GOING, FOR, SURE, THERE'S NO CONVERTING OF 'EM.

SIR THOMAS, WHITHER WERE YOU GOING?

TO THE CARDINAL'S. YOUR LORDSHIP IS A GUEST TOO.

O, 'TIS TRUE, THIS NIGHT HE MAKES A SUPPER TO MANY LORDS AND LADIES.

THAT CHURCHMAN BEARS A BOUNTEOUS MIND INDEED, A HAND AS FRUITFUL AS THE LAND THAT FEEDS US.

MEN OF HIS WAY SHOULD BE MOST LIBERAL. THEY ARE SET HERE FOR EXAMPLES.

MY BARGE STAYS, YOUR LORDSHIP SHALL ALONG.

COME, GOOD SIR THOMAS, WE SHALL BE LATE ELSE.

CARDINAL WOLSEY'S GRAND BANQUET AT YORK PLACE; AMONG THE GUESTS... ANNE BOLEYN.

SWEET LADIES, WILL IT PLEASE YOU SIT?

NAY, YOU MUST NOT FREEZE. TWO WOMEN PLACED TOGETHER MAKES COLD WEATHER.

SWEET LADIES, IF I CHANCE TO TALK A LITTLE WILD, FORGIVE ME. I HAD IT FROM MY FATHER.

WAS HE MAD, SIR?

O, VERY MAD, EXCEEDING MAD — HE WOULD KISS YOU TWENTY WITH A BREATH.

LADIES, YOU ARE NOT MERRY.

YOU'RE WELCOME, FAIR GUESTS — TO YOU ALL, GOOD HEALTH!

GENTLEMEN, WHOSE FAULT IS THIS?

THE RED WINE FIRST MUST RISE IN THEIR FAIR CHEEKS, MY LORD.

YOU ARE A MERRY GAMESTER, MY LORD SANDS.

BOOM

47

WHAT WARLIKE VOICE — AND TO WHAT END IS THIS?

NAY, LADIES, FEAR NOT.

A NOBLE TROOP OF STRANGERS HAVE LEFT THEIR BARGE AND HITHER MAKE, AS GREAT AMBASSADORS FROM FOREIGN PRINCES.

LORD CHAMBERLAIN, GIVE 'EM WELCOME — YOU CAN SPEAK THE FRENCH TONGUE.

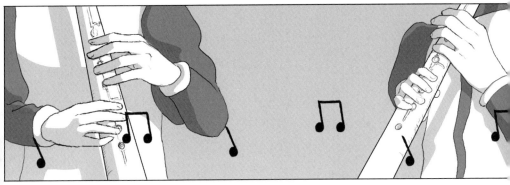

A NOBLE COMPANY! WHAT ARE THEIR PLEASURES?

HAVING HEARD BY FAME OF THIS SO FAIR ASSEMBLY, THEY CRAVE LEAVE TO VIEW THESE LADIES AND ENTREAT AN HOUR OF REVELS WITH 'EM.

THEY HAVE DONE MY POOR HOUSE GRACE.

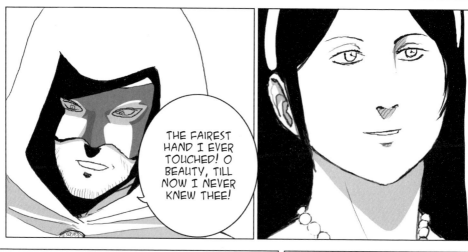

THE FAIREST HAND I EVER TOUCHED! O BEAUTY, TILL NOW I NEVER KNEW THEE!

THERE SHOULD BE ONE, BY HIS PERSON, MORE WORTHY THIS PLACE THAN MYSELF, TO WHOM I WOULD SURRENDER IT.

YE HAVE FOUND HIM, CARDINAL...

TWO GENTLEMEN MEET IN A WESTMINSTER STREET.

WHITHER AWAY SO FAST?

TO HEAR WHAT SHALL BECOME OF THE GREAT DUKE OF BUCKINGHAM.

I'LL SAVE YOU THAT LABOUR, SIR.

IS HE FOUND GUILTY?

YES, TRULY HE IS. AND CONDEMNED.

THE GREAT DUKE CAME TO THE BAR AT WHICH APPEARED AGAINST HIM HIS SURVEYOR, SIR GILBERT PARK HIS CHANCELLOR, AND JOHN COURT, CONFESSOR TO HIM, WITH THAT DEVIL MONK HOPKINS.

HE THAT FED HIM WITH HIS PROPHECIES?

THE SAME.

HIS PEERS, UPON THIS EVIDENCE, HAVE FOUND HIM GUILTY OF HIGH TREASON.

ALL THE COMMONS HATE HIM AND WISH HIM TEN FATHOM DEEP.

THIS DUKE AS MUCH THEY LOVE, AND CALL HIM "BOUNTEOUS BUCKINGHAM, THE MIRROR OF ALL COURTESY—"

STAY THERE, SIR, AND SEE THE NOBLE RUINED MAN YOU SPEAK OF.

TMM

TMM

TMM

GOOD PEOPLE, YOU THAT HAVE COME TO PITY ME, HEAR WHAT I SAY...

AND THEN GO HOME AND LOSE ME. I HAVE THIS DAY RECEIVED A TRAITOR'S JUDGEMENT AND BY THAT NAME MUST DIE. YET, HEAVEN BEAR WITNESS, EVEN AS THE AXE FALLS, IF I BE NOT FAITHFUL! THE LAW I BEAR NO MALICE FOR MY DEATH...

BUT THOSE THAT SOUGHT IT, MY GUILTLESS BLOOD MUST CRY AGAINST 'EM.

YOU FEW THAT LOVED ME, AND DARE BE BOLD TO WEEP AS THE LONG DIVORCE OF STEEL FALLS ON ME, MAKE OF YOUR PRAYERS ONE SACRIFICE, AND LIFT MY SOUL TO HEAVEN.

I DO BESEECH YOUR GRACE NOW TO FORGIVE ME FRANKLY.

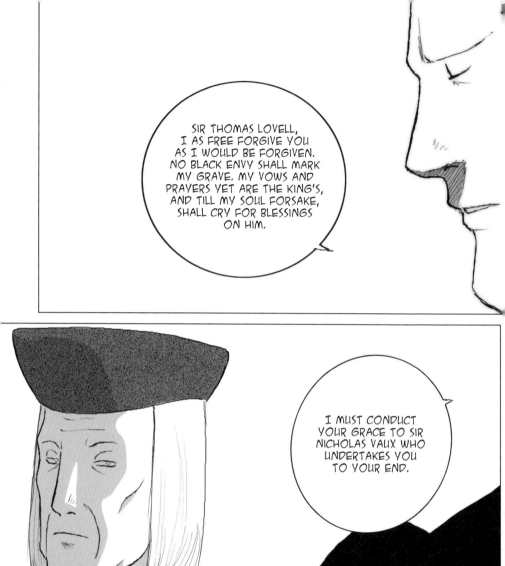

SIR THOMAS LOVELL, I AS FREE FORGIVE YOU AS I WOULD BE FORGIVEN. NO BLACK ENVY SHALL MARK MY GRAVE. MY VOWS AND PRAYERS YET ARE THE KING'S, AND TILL MY SOUL FORSAKE, SHALL CRY FOR BLESSINGS ON HIM.

I MUST CONDUCT YOUR GRACE TO SIR NICHOLAS VAUX WHO UNDERTAKES YOU TO YOUR END.

SEE THE BARGE BE FIT WITH SUCH FURNITURE AS SUITS THE GREATNESS OF HIS PERSON.

NAY, SIR NICHOLAS, LET IT ALONE. MY STATE NOW WILL BUT MOCK ME.

WHEN I CAME HITHER, I WAS LORD HIGH CONSTABLE... NOW POOR EDWARD BOHUN. YET I AM RICHER THAN MY BASE ACCUSERS THAT NEVER KNEW WHAT TRUTH MEANT.

PRAY FOR ME! THE LAST HOUR OF MY LONG WEARY LIFE IS COME UPON ME.

THAT SLANDER, SIR, GROWS AGAIN FRESHER THAN EVER IT WAS. THE CARDINAL, OUT OF MALICE TO THE GOOD QUEEN, WILL UNDO HER.

'TIS THE CARDINAL — TO REVENGE HIM ON THE EMPEROR FOR NOT BESTOWING ON HIM THE ARCHBISHOPRIC OF TOLEDO.

YOU HAVE HIT THE MARK. THE CARDINAL WILL HAVE HIS WILL, AND SHE MUST FALL.

THE DUKES OF SUFFOLK AND NORFOLK MEET WITH THE LORD CHAMBERLAIN.

HOW IS THE KING EMPLOYED?

I LEFT HIM FULL OF SAD THOUGHTS AND TROUBLES.

IT SEEMS THE MARRIAGE WITH HIS BROTHER'S WIFE HAS CREPT TOO NEAR HIS CONSCIENCE.

NO, HIS CONSCIENCE HAS CREPT TOO NEAR ANOTHER LADY.

THIS IS THE CARDINAL'S DOING, THE KING WILL KNOW HIM ONE DAY!

PRAY GOD HE DO! HE'LL NEVER KNOW HIMSELF ELSE.

NOW HE HAS CRACKED THE LEAGUE BETWEEN US AND THE EMPEROR, THE QUEEN'S NEPHEW, HE DIVES INTO THE KING'S SOUL...

AND THERE SCATTERS DOUBTS OF CONSCIENCE FOR HIS MARRIAGE. HE COUNSELS A DIVORCE, A LOSS OF HER THAT, LIKE A JEWEL, HAS HUNG TWENTY YEARS ABOUT HIS NECK.

HEAVEN WILL ONE DAY OPEN THE KING'S EYES, THAT SO LONG HAVE SLEPT UPON THIS BOLD BAD MAN.

AND FREE US FROM HIS SLAVERY.

ROME, THE NURSE OF JUDGEMENT, HATH SENT US THIS GOOD MAN, THIS LEARNED PRIEST, CARDINAL CAMPEIUS, WHOM I PRESENT UNTO YOUR HIGHNESS.

I THANK THE HOLY CONCLAVE THEY HAVE SENT ME SUCH A MAN.

TO YOUR HIGHNESS' HAND I TENDER MY COMMISSION, BY WHOSE VIRTUE, THE COURT OF ROME COMMANDING, YOU, MY LORD CARDINAL OF YORK, ARE JOINED WITH ME IN THE UNPARTIAL JUDGING OF THIS BUSINESS.

YOU ARE THE KING'S NOW.

BUT TO BE COMMANDED FOR EVER BY YOUR GRACE, WHOSE HAND HAS RAISED ME.

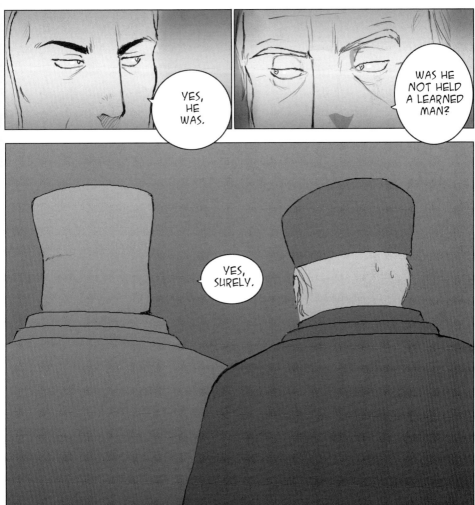

THEY SAY YOU ENVIED HIM, AND FEARING HE WOULD RISE, KEPT HIM A FOREIGN MAN, WHICH SO GRIEVED HIM THAT HE RAN MAD AND DIED.

HEAVEN'S PEACE BE WITH HIM! THAT GOOD FELLOW, IF I COMMAND HIM, FOLLOWS MY APPOINTMENT. I WILL HAVE NONE SO NEAR ELSE.

LEARN THIS, BROTHER, WE LIVE NOT TO BE GRIPPED BY MEANER PERSONS.

DELIVER THIS WITH MODESTY TO THE QUEEN.

THE MOST CONVENIENT PLACE FOR SUCH RECEIPT OF LEARNING IS BLACKFRIARS.

THERE YE SHALL MEET ABOUT THIS WEIGHTY BUSINESS. MY WOLSEY, WOULD IT NOT GRIEVE AN ABLE MAN TO LEAVE SO SWEET A BEDFELLOW? BUT, CONSCIENCE, CONSCIENCE! O, 'TIS A TENDER PLACE, AND I MUST LEAVE HER.

ANNE BOLEYN SPEAKS TO A LADY OF THE COURT.

HERE'S THE PANG THAT PINCHES...

HIS HIGHNESS HAVING LIVED SO LONG WITH HER, AND SHE NOW, AFTER GROWING IN MAJESTY...

AFTER THIS PROCESS, TO GIVE HER THE AVAUNT — IT IS A PITY WOULD MOVE A MONSTER!

HEARTS OF MOST HARD TEMPER MELT AND LAMENT FOR HER.

ALAS, POOR LADY! SHE'S A STRANGER NOW AGAIN.

MUCH BETTER SHE NEVER HAD KNOWN POMP.

...

I SWEAR, 'TIS BETTER TO BE LOWLY BORN THAN WEAR A GOLDEN SORROW.

YOU WOULD NOT BE A QUEEN?

NO, NOT FOR ALL THE RICHES UNDER HEAVEN.

'TIS STRANGE, BUT WHAT THINK YOU OF A DUCHESS? HAVE YOU LIMBS TO BEAR THAT LOAD OF TITLE?

NO, IN TRUTH.

THEN YOU ARE WEAKLY MADE. IF YOUR BACK CANNOT VOUCHSAFE THIS BURDEN, 'TIS TOO WEAK EVER TO GET A BOY.

HOW YOU DO TALK! I SWEAR AGAIN, I WOULD NOT BE A QUEEN FOR ALL THE WORLD.

WHAT WERE IT WORTH TO KNOW THE SECRET OF YOUR CONFERENCE?

IT VALUES NOT YOUR ASKING. OUR MISTRESS' SORROWS WE WERE PITYING.

SEE, SEE! I BEGGING SIXTEEN YEARS IN COURT AM YET BEGGARLY. AND YOU, A VERY FRESH FISH HERE — FIE! FIE! — HAVE YOUR MOUTH FILLED UP BEFORE YOU OPEN IT.

THIS IS STRANGE TO ME.

HOW TASTES IT? IS IT BITTER?

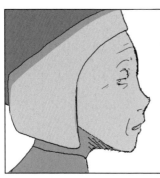

THERE WAS A LADY ONCE THAT WOULD NOT BE A QUEEN FOR ALL THE MUD IN EGYPT, HAVE YOU HEARD IT?

COME, YOU ARE PLEASANT.

THE MARCHIONESS OF PEMBROKE?

A THOUSAND POUNDS A YEAR FOR PURE RESPECT?

NO OTHER OBLIGATION?

BY MY LIFE, THAT PROMISES MORE THOUSANDS! I KNOW YOUR BACK WILL BEAR A DUCHESS. SAY, ARE YOU NOT STRONGER THAN YOU WERE?

IT FAINTS ME TO THINK WHAT FOLLOWS. THE QUEEN IS COMFORTLESS, AND WE FORGETFUL IN OUR LONG ABSENCE.

PRAY DO NOT DELIVER WHAT HERE YOU'VE HEARD TO HER.

WHAT DO YOU THINK ME?

YOU HAVE HERE, LADY, THESE REVEREND FATHERS, MEN OF INTEGRITY AND LEARNING, WHO ARE ASSEMBLED TO PLEAD YOUR CAUSE.

HIS GRACE HATH SPOKEN JUSTLY. THEREFORE, MADAM, IT'S FIT THIS ROYAL SESSION DO PROCEED WITHOUT DELAY.

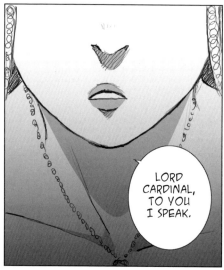

LORD CARDINAL, TO YOU I SPEAK.

YOUR PLEASURE, MADAM?

I DO BELIEVE
THAT YOU ARE MINE
ENEMY, FOR IT IS YOU
HAVE BLOWN THIS COAL
BETWIXT MY LORD
AND ME.

THEREFORE
I UTTERLY REFUSE YOU
FOR MY JUDGE, WHOM I
HOLD MY MOST MALICIOUS
FOE AND THINK NOT AT ALL
A FRIEND TO TRUTH.

MADAM,
YOU DO ME WRONG.
I HAVE NO SPLEEN AGAINST
YOU. HOW FAR I HAVE
PROCEEDED IS WARRANTED
BY A COMMISSION FROM THE
CONSISTORY OF ROME.
YOU CHARGE ME THAT
I HAVE "BLOWN THIS
COAL". I DO
DENY IT.

THE KING IS PRESENT.

IN HIM IT LIES TO REMOVE THESE THOUGHTS FROM YOU. I DO BESEECH YOU, MADAM, TO SAY SO NO MORE.

MY LORD, I AM TOO WEAK TO OPPOSE YOUR CUNNING. YOU'RE MEEK AND HUMBLE-MOUTHED, BUT YOUR HEART IS CRAMMED WITH SPLEEN AND PRIDE.

YOU HAVE, BY FORTUNE AND HIS HIGHNESS' FAVOURS, MOUNTED WHERE POWERS ARE YOUR RETAINERS.

I DO REFUSE YOU FOR MY JUDGE, AND HERE, BEFORE YOU ALL, APPEAL UNTO THE POPE, TO BRING MY WHOLE CAUSE BEFORE HIS HOLINESS AND BE JUDGED BY HIM.

THE QUEEN IS OBSTINATE. 'TIS NOT WELL. SHE'S GOING AWAY.

CALL HER AGAIN.

THEY VEX ME PAST MY PATIENCE! I WILL **NOT** TARRY, NOR EVER MORE MY APPEARANCE MAKE IN ANY OF THEIR COURTS.

GO THY WAYS, KATE, THOU ART ALONE THE QUEEN OF EARTHLY QUEENS.

MOST GRACIOUS SIR, IN HUMBLEST MANNER I REQUIRE YOUR HIGHNESS TO DECLARE WHETHER EVER I DID BROACH THIS BUSINESS TO YOUR HIGHNESS...

OR EVER SPAKE THE LEAST WORD THAT MIGHT PREJUDICE HER PRESENT STATE.

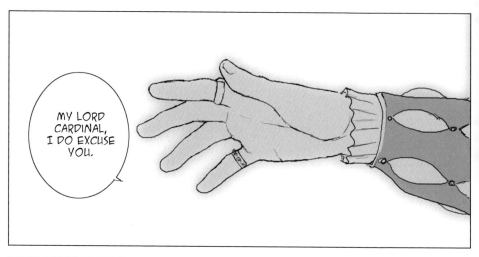

MY LORD CARDINAL, I DO EXCUSE YOU.

YOU EVER HAVE WISHED THE SLEEPING OF THIS BUSINESS, NEVER DESIRED IT TO BE STIRRED, BUT OFT HAVE HINDERED THE PASSAGES TOWARD IT.

NOW, WHAT MOVED ME TO IT? THUS IT CAME — GIVE HEED TO IT.

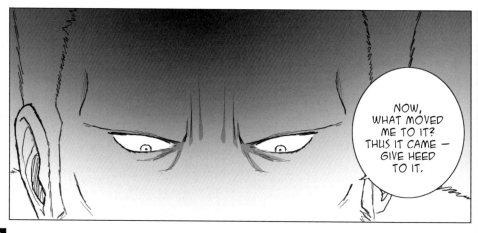

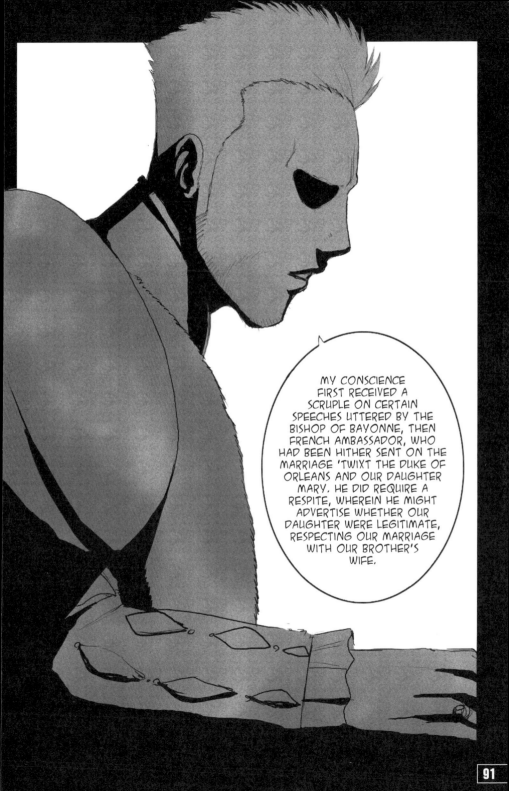

MY CONSCIENCE FIRST RECEIVED A SCRUPLE ON CERTAIN SPEECHES UTTERED BY THE BISHOP OF BAYONNE, THEN FRENCH AMBASSADOR, WHO HAD BEEN HITHER SENT ON THE MARRIAGE 'TWIXT THE DUKE OF ORLEANS AND OUR DAUGHTER MARY. HE DID REQUIRE A RESPITE, WHEREIN HE MIGHT ADVERTISE WHETHER OUR DAUGHTER WERE LEGITIMATE, RESPECTING OUR MARRIAGE WITH OUR BROTHER'S WIFE.

THIS RESPITE SHOOK THE BOSOM OF MY CONSCIENCE AND FORCED MANY MAZED CONSIDERINGS.

FIRST, METHOUGHT I STOOD NOT IN THE SMILE OF HEAVEN, WHO HAD COMMANDED THAT MY LADY'S WOMB, IF IT CONCEIVED A MALE CHILD BY ME, SHOULD DO NO MORE OFFICES OF LIFE THAN THE GRAVE DOES TO THE DEAD.

FOR HER MALE
ISSUE OR DIED WHERE
THEY WERE MADE OR SHORTLY
AFTER. HENCE I TOOK THIS
WAS A JUDGEMENT ON ME,
THAT MY KINGDOM SHOULD
NOT BE GLADDED
IN IT BY ME.

I WEIGHED THE
DANGER WHICH MY
REALMS STOOD IN BY
MY ISSUE'S FAIL, AND I
DID STEER TOWARD THIS
REMEDY WHEREUPON
WE ARE NOW PRESENT
HERE TOGETHER.

FIRST, I BEGAN IN PRIVATE WITH YOU, MY LORD OF LINCOLN, YOU REMEMBER?

VERY WELL, MY LIEGE.

THE QUESTION DID AT FIRST STAGGER ME. I COMMITTED THE DARINGEST COUNSEL AND DID ENTREAT YOUR HIGHNESS TO THIS COURSE WHICH YOU ARE RUNNING HERE.

I THEN, MY LORD OF CANTERBURY, GOT YOUR LEAVE TO MAKE THIS PRESENT SUMMONS.

I LEFT NO REVEREND PERSON IN THIS COURT, BUT BY PARTICULAR CONSENT PROCEEDED UNDER YOUR HANDS. THEREFORE, GO ON.

FOR NO DISLIKE AGAINST THE QUEEN, BUT THE THORNY POINTS OF MY ALLEGED REASONS, DRIVE THIS FORWARD.

PROVE BUT OUR MARRIAGE LAWFUL, AND WE ARE CONTENTED TO WEAR OUR MORTAL STATE WITH HER, KATHERINE OUR QUEEN.

SO PLEASE YOUR HIGHNESS, THE QUEEN BEING ABSENT, 'TIS NEEDFUL THAT WE ADJOURN THIS COURT.

MEANWHILE MUST BE AN EARNEST MOTION MADE TO THE QUEEN TO CALL BACK HER APPEAL SHE INTENDS UNTO HIS HOLINESS.

I MAY PERCEIVE THESE CARDINALS TRIFLE WITH ME.

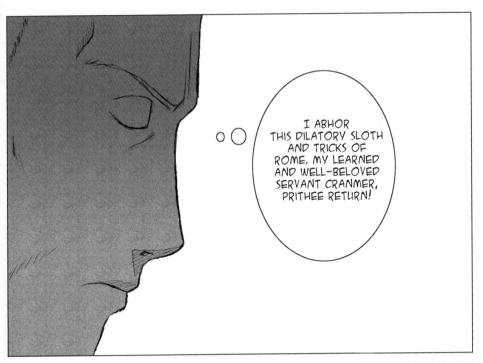

I ABHOR THIS DILATORY SLOTH AND TRICKS OF ROME, MY LEARNED AND WELL-BELOVED SERVANT CRANMER, PRITHEE RETURN!

WITH THY APPROACH, I KNOW MY COMFORT COMES ALONG.

TAKE THY LUTE, WENCH. MY SOUL GROWS SAD WITH TROUBLES.

SING, AND DISPERSE 'EM, IF THOU CANST.

ORPHEUS WITH HIS LUTE MADE TREES, AND THE MOUNTAIN TOPS THAT FREEZE, BOW THEMSELVES WHEN HE DID SING...

KNOCK KNOCK

HOW NOW!

YOUR GRACE, THE TWO GREAT CARDINALS WAIT IN THE PRESENCE.

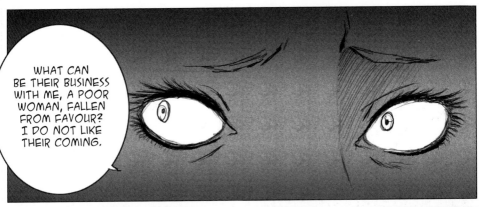

WHAT CAN BE THEIR BUSINESS WITH ME, A POOR WOMAN, FALLEN FROM FAVOUR? I DO NOT LIKE THEIR COMING.

PEACE TO YOUR HIGHNESS!

WHAT ARE YOUR PLEASURES WITH ME, REVEREND LORDS?

MAY IT PLEASE YOU, MADAM, TO WITHDRAW INTO YOUR PRIVATE CHAMBER? WE SHALL GIVE YOU THE FULL CAUSE OF OUR COMING.

SPEAK IT HERE. THERE'S NOTHING I HAVE DONE YET, ON MY CONSCIENCE, DESERVES A CORNER.

IF YOUR BUSINESS SEEK ME OUT, AND THAT WAY I AM WIFE IN, OUT WITH IT BOLDLY. TRUTH LOVES OPEN DEALING.

TANTA EST ERGA TE MENTIS INTEGRITAS, REGINA SERENISSIMA —

MY LORD, NO LATIN! A STRANGE TONGUE MAKES MY CAUSE MORE SUSPICIOUS.

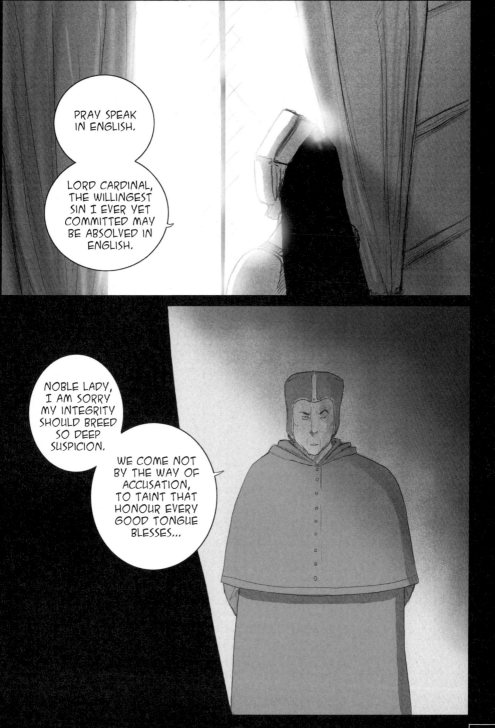

ALAS, I AM A WOMAN FRIENDLESS, HOPELESS!

MADAM, YOU WRONG THE KING'S LOVE WITH THESE FEARS. YOUR HOPES AND FRIENDS ARE INFINITE.

BUT LITTLE FOR MY PROFIT. CAN YOU THINK THAT ANY ENGLISHMAN DARE GIVE ME COUNSEL? OR BE A KNOWN FRIEND AGAINST HIS HIGHNESS' PLEASURE, AND LIVE A SUBJECT?

NAY, MY FRIENDS LIVE NOT HERE. THEY ARE FAR HENCE IN MINE OWN COUNTRY.

PUT YOUR MAIN CAUSE INTO THE KING'S PROTECTION. 'TWILL MUCH BETTER YOUR CAUSE. FOR IF THE TRIAL OF THE LAW OVERTAKE YE, YOU'LL PART AWAY DISGRACED.

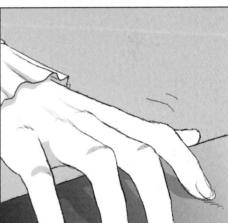

HE TELLS YOU RIGHTLY.

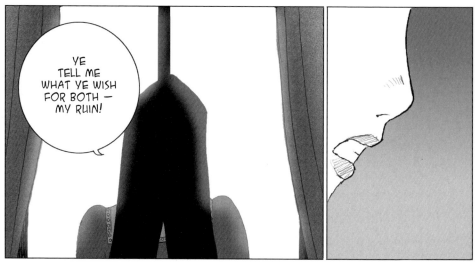

HAVE I LIVED
THUS LONG —
A WIFE, A TRUE ONE...
A WOMAN NEVER YET
BRANDED WITH
SUSPICION... AND AM I
THUS REWARDED?
'TIS NOT WELL,
LORDS.

MADAM, YOU
WANDER FROM
THE GOOD WE
AIM AT.

MY LORD, I DARE NOT MAKE MYSELF SO GUILTY TO GIVE UP WILLINGLY THAT NOBLE TITLE YOUR MASTER WED ME TO. NOTHING BUT DEATH SHALL EVER DIVORCE MY DIGNITIES.

PRAY HEAR ME.

WOULD I HAD NEVER TROD THIS ENGLISH EARTH, OR FELT THE FLATTERIES THAT GROW UPON IT! YE HAVE ANGELS' FACES, BUT HEAVEN KNOWS YOUR HEARTS.

DO WHAT YE WILL, MY LORDS, AND, PRAY FORGIVE ME.

HIS MAJESTY HAS MY HEART YET, AND SHALL HAVE MY PRAYERS WHILE I SHALL HAVE MY LIFE.

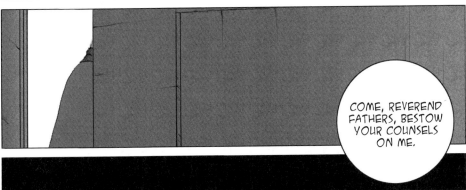

COME, REVEREND FATHERS, BESTOW YOUR COUNSELS ON ME.

IF YOU WILL NOW UNITE IN YOUR COMPLAINTS, THE CARDINAL CANNOT STAND UNDER THEM.

MY LORDS, I MUCH FEAR. IF YOU CANNOT BAR HIS ACCESS TO THE KING, NEVER ATTEMPT ANYTHING ON HIM.

FOR HE HATH A WITCHCRAFT OVER THE KING IN HIS TONGUE.

O, FEAR HIM NOT. HIS SPELL IN THAT IS OUT. THE KING HATH FOUND MATTER AGAINST HIM.

WILL THIS WORK?

THE KING IN THIS PERCEIVES HOW HE HEDGES HIS OWN WAY.

ALL HIS TRICKS FOUNDER. THE KING ALREADY HATH MARRIED THE FAIR LADY.

THERE'S ORDER GIVEN FOR HER CORONATION, FROM HER WILL FALL SOME BLESSING TO THIS LAND.

BUT WILL THE KING DIGEST THIS LETTER OF THE CARDINAL'S? THE LORD FORBID!

BUT WHEN RETURNS CRANMER?

HE IS RETURNED IN HIS OPINIONS, WHICH HAVE SATISFIED THE KING FOR HIS DIVORCE. SHORTLY, HIS SECOND MARRIAGE SHALL BE PUBLISHED AND HER CORONATION.

KATHERINE NO MORE SHALL BE CALLED "QUEEN" BUT "PRINCESS DOWAGER" AND "WIDOW TO PRINCE ARTHUR".

THIS CRANMER'S A WORTHY FELLOW, AND HATH TAKEN MUCH PAIN IN THE KING'S BUSINESS.

HE HAS, AND WE SHALL SEE HIM FOR IT AN ARCHBISHOP.

THE CARDINAL!

OBSERVE, OBSERVE — HE'S MOODY.

THE PACKET, CROMWELL, GAVE IT YOU THE KING?

TO HIS OWN HAND.

HE DID UNSEAL THEM, AND THE FIRST HE VIEWED WITH A SERIOUS MIND.

IS HE READY TO COME?

I THINK HE IS.

HE IS VEXED AT SOMETHING.

THE KING, THE KING!

WHAT PILES OF WEALTH HATH HE ACCUMULATED TO HIS OWN PORTION!

HOW, IN THE NAME OF THRIFT, DOES HE RAKE THIS TOGETHER?

NOW, MY LORDS, SAW YOU THE CARDINAL?

MY LORD, WE HAVE STOOD HERE OBSERVING HIM. SOME STRANGE COMMOTION IS IN HIS BRAIN.

IT MAY WELL BE. THERE IS A MUTINY IN HIS MIND. THIS MORNING, PAPERS OF STATE HE SENT ME AS I REQUIRED. I FOUND THERE AN INVENTORY OF HIS TREASURE, AT SUCH PROUD RATE THAT IT OUT-SPEAKS POSSESSION OF A SUBJECT.

IT'S HEAVEN'S WILL PUT THIS PAPER IN THE PACKET TO BLESS YOUR EYE.

SINCE I HAD MY OFFICE, I HAVE NOT ALONE EMPLOYED YOU WHERE HIGH PROFITS MIGHT COME HOME, BUT PARED MY PRESENT HAVINGS TO BESTOW MY BOUNTIES UPON YOU.

EVER GOD BLESS YOUR HIGHNESS!

WHAT SHOULD THIS MEAN?

125

HAVE I NOT MADE YOU THE PRIME MAN OF THE STATE?

I CONFESS YOUR ROYAL GRACES, SHOWERED ON ME DAILY, HAVE BEEN MORE THAN COULD MY PURPOSES REQUITE. MINE OWN ENDS HAVE POINTED TO THE GOOD OF YOUR MOST SACRED PERSON AND THE PROFIT OF THE STATE. MY LOYALTY EVER HAS AND EVER SHALL BE GROWING, TILL DEATH KILL IT.

FAIRLY ANSWERED.
MY HAND HAS OPENED
BOUNTY TO YOU, MY
HEART DROPPED LOVE, MY
POWER RAINED HONOUR,
MORE ON YOU THAN ANY.
SO YOUR HAND AND HEART,
YOUR BRAIN, AND EVERY
FUNCTION OF YOUR POWER,
SHOULD BE MORE TO ME
THAN ANY.

I DO PROFESS THAT FOR YOUR HIGHNESS' GOOD I EVER LABOURED MORE THAN MINE OWN.

'TIS NOBLY SPOKEN.

TAKE NOTICE, LORDS, HE HAS A LOYAL BREAST, FOR YOU HAVE SEEN HIM OPEN IT.

READ OVER THIS...

AND, AFTER THIS, THEN TO BREAKFAST WITH WHAT APPETITE YOU HAVE.

WHAT SUDDEN ANGER'S THIS?

HE PARTED FROWNING FROM ME, AS IF RUIN LEAPED FROM HIS EYES.

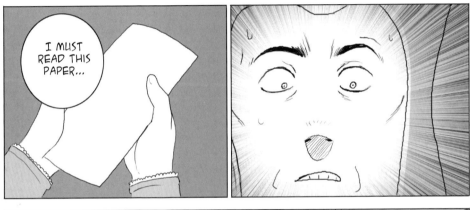

I MUST READ THIS PAPER...

THIS PAPER HAS UNDONE ME! 'TIS THE ACCOUNT OF ALL THAT WEALTH I HAVE DRAWN TOGETHER FOR MINE OWN ENDS — INDEED, TO GAIN THE POPEDOM.

O NEGLIGENCE! WHAT DEVIL MADE ME PUT THIS SECRET IN THE PACKET I SENT THE KING?

IS THERE NO WAY TO CURE THIS?

YET I KNOW A WAY, IN SPITE OF FORTUNE, WILL BRING ME OFF AGAIN.

WHAT'S THIS? "TO THE POPE"!

THE LETTER WITH ALL THE BUSINESS I WRIT TO HIS HOLINESS.

NAY THEN, FAREWELL! I HAVE TOUCHED THE HIGHEST POINT OF ALL MY GREATNESS... AND FROM THAT FULL MERIDIAN OF MY GLORY, I HASTE NOW TO MY SETTING.

I SHALL FALL LIKE A BRIGHT EXHALATION IN THE EVENING, AND NO MAN SEE ME MORE.

HEAR THE KING'S PLEASURE, CARDINAL, WHO COMMANDS YOU TO RENDER UP THE GREAT SEAL INTO OUR HANDS...

AND TO CONFINE YOURSELF TO ESHER HOUSE TILL YOU HEAR FURTHER FROM HIS HIGHNESS.

WHERE'S YOUR COMMISSION, LORDS? WORDS CANNOT CARRY AUTHORITY SO WEIGHTY.

THAT SEAL YOU ASK WITH SUCH VIOLENCE, THE KING WITH HIS OWN HAND GAVE ME. NOW, WHO'LL TAKE IT?

THE KING THAT GAVE IT.

IT MUST BE HIMSELF, THEN.

THOU ART A PROUD TRAITOR, PRIEST. MY LORD OF NORFOLK, PRODUCE THE GRAND SUM OF HIS SINS, THE ARTICLES COLLECTED FROM HIS LIFE.

THOSE ARTICLES, MY LORD, ARE IN THE KING'S HAND.

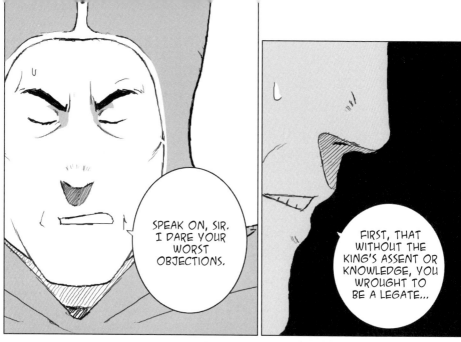

SPEAK ON, SIR. I DARE YOUR WORST OBJECTIONS.

FIRST, THAT WITHOUT THE KING'S ASSENT OR KNOWLEDGE, YOU WROUGHT TO BE A LEGATE...

BY WHICH POWER YOU MAIMED THE JURISDICTION OF ALL BISHOPS.

THEN, THAT IN ALL YOU WRIT TO ROME, OR ELSE TO FOREIGN PRINCES, YOU BROUGHT THE KING TO BE YOUR SERVANT.

THEN, THAT WITHOUT THE KNOWLEDGE EITHER OF KING OR COUNCIL, YOU WENT AMBASSADOR TO THE EMPEROR.

THAT, OUT OF MERE AMBITION, YOU HAVE CAUSED YOUR HOLY HAT TO BE STAMPED ON THE KING'S COIN.

THEN, THAT YOU HAVE SENT INNUMERABLE SUBSTANCE TO FURNISH ROME AND PREPARE THE WAYS YOU HAVE FOR DIGNITIES. MANY MORE THERE ARE, WHICH I WILL NOT TAINT MY MOUTH WITH.

O MY LORD, PRESS NOT A FALLING MAN TOO FAR! HIS FAULTS LIE OPEN TO THE LAWS. LET THEM CORRECT HIM.

MY HEART WEEPS TO SEE HIM SO LITTLE OF HIS GREAT SELF.

THE KING'S FURTHER PLEASURE IS THAT A WRIT BE SUED AGAINST YOU TO FORFEIT ALL YOUR GOODS, LANDS AND WHATSOEVER, AND TO BE OUT OF THE KING'S PROTECTION.

THIS IS MY CHARGE.

FOR YOUR STUBBORN ANSWER ABOUT THE GIVING BACK THE GREAT SEAL TO US, THE KING SHALL KNOW IT, AND, NO DOUBT, SHALL THANK YOU.

SO FARE YOU WELL, MY LITTLE GOOD LORD CARDINAL.

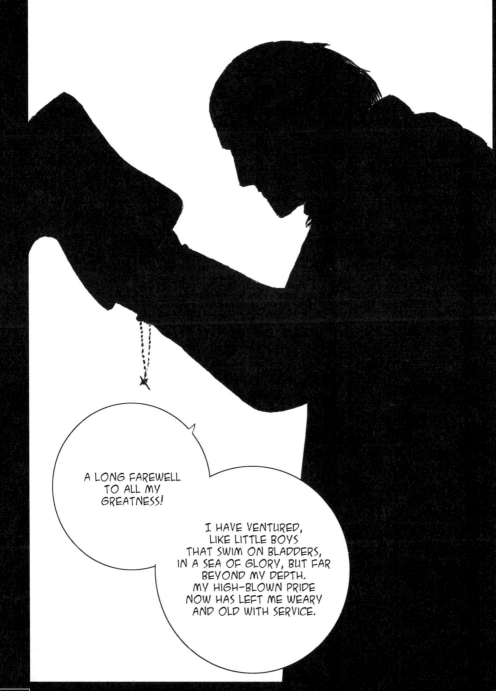

VAIN POMP AND GLORY OF THIS WORLD, I HATE YE!

O, HOW WRETCHED IS THAT POOR MAN THAT HANGS ON PRINCES' FAVOURS!

THERE IS, BETWIXT THAT SMILE OF PRINCES AND THEIR RUIN, MORE PANGS AND FEARS THAN WARS HAVE.

AND WHEN HE FALLS, HE FALLS LIKE LUCIFER, NEVER TO HOPE AGAIN.

WHY, HOW NOW, CROMWELL?

I HAVE NO POWER TO SPEAK, SIR.

WHAT, AMAZED AT MY MISFORTUNES? CAN THY SPIRIT WONDER A GREAT MAN SHOULD DECLINE?

HOW DOES YOUR GRACE?

WHY, WELL.
NEVER SO TRULY HAPPY.
I KNOW MYSELF NOW, AND
I FEEL WITHIN ME A PEACE
ABOVE ALL EARTHLY
DIGNITIES.

THE KING HAS
TAKEN A LOAD
WOULD SINK A NAVY.
O, 'TIS A BURDEN,
CROMWELL, TOO
HEAVY FOR A MAN
THAT HOPES FOR
HEAVEN!

I AM GLAD
YOUR GRACE HAS
MADE THAT RIGHT
USE OF IT.

THAT'S SOMEWHAT SUDDEN, BUT HE'S A LEARNED MAN. MAY HE CONTINUE LONG IN HIS HIGHNESS' FAVOUR AND DO JUSTICE FOR TRUTH'S SAKE. WHAT MORE?

THAT CRANMER IS INSTALLED LORD ARCHBISHOP OF CANTERBURY.

THAT'S NEWS INDEED.

LAST, THAT THE LADY ANNE, WHOM THE KING HATH IN SECRECY LONG MARRIED, THIS DAY WAS VIEWED IN OPEN AS HIS QUEEN.

THE VOICE IS NOW ONLY ABOUT HER CORONATION.

THERE WAS THE WEIGHT THAT PULLED ME DOWN. ALL MY GLORIES IN THAT ONE WOMAN I HAVE LOST FOR EVER.

GO FROM ME, CROMWELL.

FLING AWAY AMBITION. BY THAT SIN FELL THE ANGELS. LET ALL THE ENDS THOU AIM'ST AT BE THY COUNTRY'S.

THEN IF THOU FALL'ST, THOU FALL'ST A BLESSED MARTYR!

O CROMWELL! HAD I BUT SERVED MY GOD WITH HALF THE ZEAL I SERVED MY KING, HE WOULD NOT HAVE LEFT ME NAKED TO MINE ENEMIES.

WHAT CONTAINS THAT PAPER IN YOUR HAND?

'TIS THE LIST OF THOSE THAT CLAIM THEIR OFFICES THIS DAY BY CUSTOM OF THE CORONATION. THE DUKE OF SUFFOLK IS THE FIRST, AND CLAIMS TO BE HIGH STEWARD.

NEXT, THE DUKE OF NORFOLK, EARL MARSHAL. YOU MAY READ THE REST.

WHAT'S BECOME OF KATHERINE, THE PRINCESS DOWAGER? HOW GOES HER BUSINESS?

THE ARCHBISHOP OF CANTERBURY, WITH OTHER REVEREND FATHERS, HELD A COURT. BY ASSENT OF ALL THESE LEARNED MEN, SHE WAS DIVORCED.

SINCE WHICH SHE WAS REMOVED TO KIMBOLTON, WHERE SHE REMAINS NOW SICK.

ALAS, GOOD LADY!

THE CORONATION OF ANNE BOLEYN.

GOD SAVE YOU, SIR! WHERE HAVE YOU BEEN BROILING?

AMONG THE CROWD IN THE ABBEY WHERE A FINGER COULD NOT BE WEDGED IN MORE.

YOU SAW THE CEREMONY?

HOW WAS IT?

WELL WORTH THE SEEING.

HER GRACE CAME TO THE ALTAR, WHERE SHE KNEELED, CAST HER FAIR EYES TO HEAVEN, AND PRAYED DEVOUTLY.

SHE HAD THE HOLY OIL, EDWARD CONFESSOR'S CROWN, THE ROD AND BIRD OF PEACE, AND ALL SUCH EMBLEMS LAID NOBLY ON HER.

SO SHE PACED BACK AGAIN TO YORK PLACE WHERE THE FEAST IS HELD.

153

WHAT TWO REVEREND BISHOPS WERE THOSE THAT WENT ON EACH SIDE OF THE QUEEN?

STOKESLEY AND GARDINER, THE ONE OF WINCHESTER, NEWLY PREFERRED FROM THE KING'S SECRETARY, THE OTHER, LONDON.

HE OF WINCHESTER IS HELD NO GREAT GOOD LOVER OF ARCHBISHOP CRANMER.

ALL THE LAND KNOWS THAT.

YET THERE IS NO GREAT BREACH.

WHEN IT COMES, CRANMER WILL FIND A FRIEND WILL NOT SHRINK FROM HIM.

WHO MAY THAT BE?

THOMAS CROMWELL.

THE KING HAS MADE HIM MASTER OF THE JEWEL HOUSE AND ONE OF THE PRIVY COUNCIL.

HE WILL DESERVE MORE.

YES, WITHOUT DOUBT.

COME, GENTLEMEN, YE SHALL GO MY WAY, WHICH IS TO THE COURT.

THERE YE SHALL BE MY GUESTS.

HOW DOES YOUR GRACE?

O GRIFFITH, SICK TO DEATH!

MY LEGS, LIKE LOADEN BRANCHES, BOW TO THE EARTH.

DIDST THOU NOT TELL ME THAT CARDINAL WOLSEY WAS DEAD?

YES, MADAM.

TELL ME HOW HE DIED. IF WELL, HE STEPPED BEFORE ME HAPPILY FOR MY EXAMPLE.

WELL, THE VOICE GOES, MADAM. FOR AFTER THE EARL NORTHUMBERLAND ARRESTED HIM AT YORK, HE FELL SICK SUDDENLY.

ALAS, POOR MAN!

THREE NIGHTS AFTER THIS, ABOUT THE HOUR OF EIGHT, WHICH HE HIMSELF FORETOLD SHOULD BE HIS LAST, FULL OF REPENTANCE, HE GAVE HIS BLESSED PART TO HEAVEN, AND SLEPT IN PEACE.

SO MAY HE REST. HIS FAULTS LIE GENTLY ON HIM.

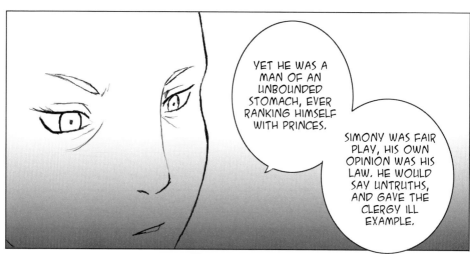

YET HE WAS A MAN OF AN UNBOUNDED STOMACH, EVER RANKING HIMSELF WITH PRINCES.

SIMONY WAS FAIR PLAY, HIS OWN OPINION WAS HIS LAW. HE WOULD SAY UNTRUTHS, AND GAVE THE CLERGY ILL EXAMPLE.

MEN'S EVIL MANNERS LIVE IN BRASS, THEIR VIRTUES WE WRITE IN WATER.

MAY IT PLEASE YOUR HIGHNESS TO HEAR ME SPEAK HIS GOOD NOW?

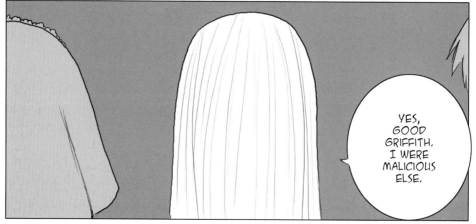

YES, GOOD GRIFFITH. I WERE MALICIOUS ELSE.

THE OTHER, YET SO FAMOUS, SO EXCELLENT IN ART, THAT CHRISTENDOM SHALL EVER SPEAK HIS VIRTUE.

HIS OVERTHROW HEAPED HAPPINESS UPON HIM, AND HE DIED FEARING GOD.

AFTER MY DEATH I WISH NO OTHER HERALD BUT SUCH AN HONEST CHRONICLER AS GRIFFITH.

PEACE BE WITH HIM!

PATIENCE, BE NEAR ME STILL. I HAVE NOT LONG TO TROUBLE THEE.

GOOD GRIFFITH, CAUSE THE MUSICIANS PLAY ME THAT SAD NOTE I NAMED MY KNELL...

WHILST I SIT MEDITATING ON THAT CELESTIAL HARMONY I GO TO.

SHE IS ASLEEP. LET'S SIT DOWN QUIET, FOR FEAR WE WAKE HER.

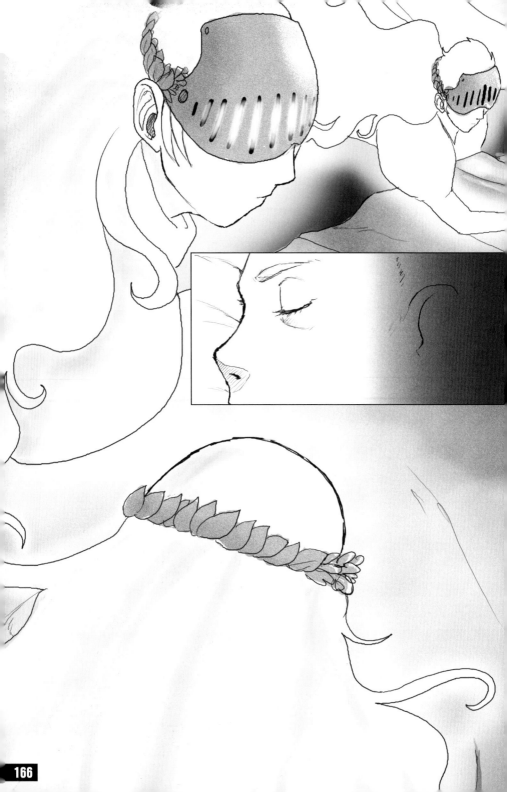

SPIRITS OF PEACE, WHERE ARE YE?

ARE YE ALL GONE, AND LEAVE ME HERE IN WRETCHEDNESS?

MADAM, WE ARE HERE.

IT IS NOT YOU I CALL FOR.

SAW YE NONE ENTER SINCE I SLEPT?

NONE, MADAM.

168

NO? SAW YOU NOT A BLESSED TROOP WHOSE BRIGHT FACES CAST THOUSAND BEAMS UPON ME, LIKE THE SUN? THEY PROMISED ME ETERNAL HAPPINESS.

I AM MOST JOYFUL, MADAM, SUCH GOOD DREAMS POSSESS YOUR FANCY.

DO YOU NOTE HOW MUCH HER GRACE IS ALTERED? HOW PALE SHE LOOKS, AND OF AN EARTHY COLD?

SHE IS GOING, WENCH. PRAY, PRAY.

YOU ARE A SAUCY FELLOW. DESERVE WE NO MORE REVERENCE?

GO TO – KNEEL!

THERE IS A GENTLEMAN, SENT FROM THE KING, TO SEE YOU.

IF MY SIGHT FAIL NOT, YOU SHOULD BE LORD AMBASSADOR FROM THE EMPEROR, MY ROYAL NEPHEW, AND YOUR NAME CAPUCIUS.

THE KING GRIEVES MUCH FOR YOUR WEAKNESS, AND HEARTILY ENTREATS YOU TAKE GOOD COMFORT.

THAT COMFORT COMES TOO LATE.

'TIS LIKE A PARDON AFTER EXECUTION.

SIR, I PRAY YOU TO DELIVER THIS TO MY LORD THE KING.

I HAVE COMMENDED TO HIS GOODNESS HIS YOUNG DAUGHTER, BESEECHING HIM TO GIVE HER VIRTUOUS BREEDING.

I HOPE SHE WILL DESERVE WELL, AND A LITTLE FOR HER MOTHER'S SAKE, THAT LOVED HIM, HEAVEN KNOWS HOW DEARLY.

MY NEXT PETITION IS THAT HIS NOBLE GRACE HAVE SOME PITY UPON MY WRETCHED WOMEN, THAT SO LONG HAVE FOLLOWED BOTH MY FORTUNES FAITHFULLY.

THE LAST IS FOR MY MEN — THEY ARE THE POOREST — THAT THEY MAY HAVE THEIR WAGES DULY PAID 'EM, AND SOMETHING OVER TO REMEMBER ME BY.

AS YOU WISH CHRISTIAN PEACE TO SOULS DEPARTED, STAND THESE POOR PEOPLE'S FRIEND, AND URGE THE KING TO DO ME THIS LAST RIGHT.

BY HEAVEN, I WILL.

REMEMBER ME IN ALL HUMILITY UNTO HIS HIGHNESS.

SAY HIS LONG TROUBLE NOW IS PASSING OUT OF THIS WORLD.

MINE EYES GROW DIM. FAREWELL.

WHEN I AM DEAD, STREW ME OVER WITH MAIDEN FLOWERS, THAT ALL THE WORLD MAY KNOW I WAS A CHASTE WIFE TO MY GRAVE.

EMBALM ME, THEN LAY ME FORTH YET LIKE A QUEEN, AND DAUGHTER TO A KING.

SIR THOMAS LOVELL, WHAT'S THE MATTER?

IT SEEMS YOU ARE IN HASTE.

AFFAIRS THAT WALK, AS THEY SAY SPIRITS DO AT MIDNIGHT, HAVE A WILDER NATURE THAN THE BUSINESS THAT SEEKS DISPATCH BY DAY.

MY LORD, I COMMEND A SECRET TO YOUR EAR. THE QUEEN'S IN LABOUR...

IN GREAT EXTREMITY, AND FEARED SHE'LL WITH THE LABOUR END.

THE FRUIT SHE GOES WITH, I PRAY THAT IT MAY LIVE. BUT FOR THE STOCK, I WISH IT GRUBBED UP NOW.

METHINKS I COULD CRY AMEN.

AND YET MY CONSCIENCE SAYS SHE, SWEET LADY, DOES DESERVE OUR BETTER WISHES.

LET ME TELL YOU, IT WILL NEVER BE WELL TILL CRANMER, CROMWELL AND SHE SLEEP IN THEIR GRAVES.

YOU SPEAK OF TWO THE MOST REMARKED IN THE KINGDOM.

CROMWELL IS THE KING'S SECRETARY.

THE ARCHBISHOP IS THE KING'S HAND AND TONGUE, AND WHO DARE SPEAK ONE SYLLABLE AGAINST HIM?

YES, YES, THERE ARE THAT DARE.

I MYSELF HAVE VENTURED TO SPEAK MY MIND OF HIM, THAT HE IS A MOST ARCH HERETIC, A PESTILENCE THAT DOES INFECT THE LAND.

THE KING, WHO
HATH SO FAR GIVEN
EAR TO OUR
COMPLAINT, HATH
COMMANDED
TOMORROW
MORNING TO THE
COUNCIL BOARD HE
BE CONVENTED.

HE'S A
RANK WEED,
AND WE MUST
ROOT HIM
OUT.

I HINDER
YOU TOO
LONG. GOOD
NIGHT, SIR
THOMAS.

NOW, LOVELL, FROM THE QUEEN WHAT IS THE NEWS?

I COULD NOT PERSONALLY DELIVER TO HER WHAT YOU COMMANDED ME.

BUT HER WOMAN RETURNED HER THANKS AND DESIRED YOUR HIGHNESS MOST HEARTILY TO PRAY FOR HER.

HA? TO PRAY FOR HER? WHAT, IS SHE CRYING OUT?

SO SAID HER WOMAN, AND THAT HER SUFFERANCE MADE ALMOST EACH PANG A DEATH.

ALAS, GOOD LADY!

GOD SAFELY QUIT HER OF HER BURDEN, AND TO THE GLADDING OF YOUR HIGHNESS WITH AN HEIR!

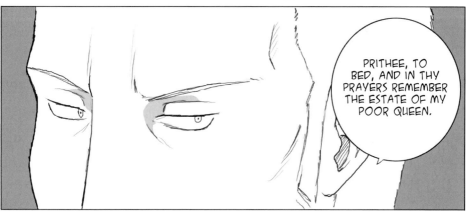

PRITHEE, TO BED, AND IN THY PRAYERS REMEMBER THE ESTATE OF MY POOR QUEEN.

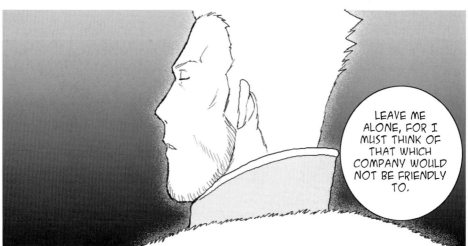

LEAVE ME ALONE, FOR I MUST THINK OF THAT WHICH COMPANY WOULD NOT BE FRIENDLY TO.

I KNOW YOU CANNOT WITH SUCH FREEDOM PURGE YOURSELF.

BUT, TILL FURTHER TRIAL WILL REQUIRE YOUR ANSWER, YOU MUST BE WELL CONTENTED TO MAKE YOUR HOUSE OUR TOWER.

IT FITS WE THUS PROCEED, OR ELSE NO WITNESS WOULD COME AGAINST YOU.

I KNOW THERE'S NONE STANDS UNDER MORE CALUMNIOUS TONGUES THAN I MYSELF.

STAND UP, GOOD CANTERBURY. WHAT MANNER OF MAN ARE YOU?

I LOOKED YOU WOULD HAVE GIVEN ME YOUR PETITION, THAT I SHOULD BRING TOGETHER YOURSELF AND YOUR ACCUSERS, AND HEARD YOU WITHOUT ENDURANCE FURTHER.

THE GOOD I STAND ON IS MY TRUTH AND HONESTY.

I FEAR NOTHING WHAT CAN BE SAID AGAINST ME.

GOD AND YOUR MAJESTY PROTECT MINE INNOCENCE, OR I FALL INTO THE TRAP IS LAID FOR ME!

BE OF GOOD CHEER, THEY SHALL NO MORE PREVAIL THAN WE GIVE WAY TO. THIS MORNING SEE YOU DO APPEAR BEFORE THEM.

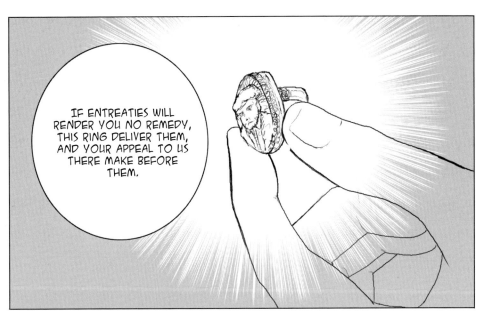

IF ENTREATIES WILL RENDER YOU NO REMEDY, THIS RING DELIVER THEM, AND YOUR APPEAL TO US THERE MAKE BEFORE THEM.

LOOK, THE GOOD MAN WEEPS! I SWEAR HE IS TRUE-HEARTED.

GET YOU GONE AND DO AS I HAVE BID YOU.

NOW BY THY LOOKS I GUESS THY MESSAGE.

IS THE QUEEN DELIVERED? AND OF A BOY?

'TIS A GIRL, PROMISES BOYS HEREAFTER.

SIR, YOUR QUEEN DESIRES YOUR VISITATION, AND TO BE ACQUAINTED WITH THIS STRANGER. 'TIS AS LIKE YOU AS CHERRY IS TO CHERRY.

GIVE HER AN HUNDRED MARKS. I'LL TO THE QUEEN.

ARCHBISHOP CRANMER STANDS ACCUSED BY HIS PEERS.

MY GOOD LORD ARCHBISHOP, I'M VERY SORRY TO SIT HERE AND BEHOLD THAT CHAIR STAND EMPTY.

BUT YOU, THAT BEST SHOULD TEACH US, HAVE MISDEMEANED YOURSELF...

TOWARD THE KING FIRST, THEN HIS LAWS, BY TEACHING HERESIES.

IF WE SUFFER THIS CONTAGIOUS SICKNESS, WHAT FOLLOWS THEN?

COMMOTIONS OF THE WHOLE STATE, AS GERMANY CAN DEARLY WITNESS.

I DO BESEECH YOUR LORDSHIPS THAT IN THIS CASE, OF JUSTICE, MY ACCUSERS STAND FORTH FACE TO FACE AND FREELY URGE AGAINST ME.

NAY, MY LORD, THAT CANNOT BE. YOU ARE A COUNCILLOR, AND BY THAT VIRTUE NO MAN DARE ACCUSE YOU.

'TIS HIS HIGHNESS' PLEASURE, FOR BETTER TRIAL OF YOU, FROM HENCE YOU BE COMMITTED TO THE TOWER... WHERE, BEING BUT A PRIVATE MAN AGAIN, YOU SHALL KNOW MANY DARE ACCUSE YOU BOLDLY.

THIS IS TOO MUCH. FORBEAR, FOR SHAME, MY LORDS.

THEN THUS IT STANDS AGREED BY ALL THAT FORTHWITH YOU BE CONVEYED TO THE TOWER A PRISONER... THERE TO REMAIN TILL THE KING'S FURTHER PLEASURE BE KNOWN UNTO US.

IS THERE NO OTHER WAY OF MERCY BUT I MUST NEEDS TO THE TOWER?

WHAT OTHER WOULD YOU EXPECT? YOU ARE STRANGELY TROUBLESOME.

STAY, I HAVE A LITTLE YET TO SAY. LOOK THERE, MY LORDS.

BY VIRTUE OF THAT RING, I TAKE MY CAUSE OUT OF THE GRIPES OF CRUEL MEN, AND GIVE IT TO A MOST NOBLE JUDGE, THE KING MY MASTER.

THIS IS THE KING'S RING.

BY HEAVEN, I TOLD YE ALL, WHEN YE FIRST PUT THIS DANGEROUS STONE A-ROLLING, 'TWOULD FALL UPON OURSELVES.

DO YOU THINK, MY LORDS, THE KING WILL SUFFER BUT THE LITTLE FINGER OF THIS MAN TO BE VEXED?

'TIS NOW TOO CERTAIN.

YE BLEW THE FIRE THAT BURNS YE. NOW HAVE AT YE!

MAY IT PLEASE YOUR GRACE —

NO, SIR, IT DOES NOT PLEASE ME.

I THOUGHT I HAD MEN OF SOME UNDERSTANDING AND WISDOM OF MY COUNCIL, BUT I FIND NONE.

I GAVE YE POWER TO TRY HIM. THERE'S SOME OF YE, I SEE, MORE OUT OF MALICE THAN INTEGRITY, WOULD TRY HIM TO THE UTMOST, HAD YE MEAN...

WHICH YE SHALL NEVER HAVE WHILE I LIVE.

THE BAPTISM OF ELIZABETH, DAUGHTER OF HENRY VIII AND QUEEN ANNE.

HEAVEN SEND PROSPEROUS LIFE, LONG AND EVER HAPPY, TO THE PRINCESS OF ENGLAND, ELIZABETH!

THIS ROYAL INFANT PROMISES UPON THIS LAND A THOUSAND BLESSINGS.

IN HER DAYS, EVERY MAN SHALL EAT IN SAFETY WHAT HE PLANTS, AND SING SONGS OF PEACE TO ALL HIS NEIGHBOURS.

AS WHEN THE MAIDEN PHOENIX DIES, HER ASHES NEW CREATE ANOTHER HEIR, SO SHALL SHE LEAVE HER BLESSEDNESS TO ONE WHO FROM THE SACRED ASHES OF HER HONOUR SHALL STAR-LIKE RISE AS GREAT IN FAME AS SHE WAS.

THOU SPEAKEST WONDERS, LORD ARCHBISHOP.

THIS ORACLE OF COMFORT HAS SO PLEASED ME, THAT WHEN I AM IN HEAVEN I SHALL DESIRE TO SEE WHAT THIS CHILD DOES, AND PRAISE MY MAKER. I THANK YE ALL. LEAD THE WAY, LORDS.

THE END

THRONE OF BLOOD

QUEEN ELIZABETH I REIGNED FROM 1558 TO 1603, A "GOLDEN AGE" OF SORTS, BUT ONE THAT CAME PAVED BY BLOOD. IN 1536, BEFORE HER THIRD BIRTHDAY, HER MOTHER ANNE BOLEYN WAS EXECUTED FOR TREASON.

I WAS ACCUSED OF ADULTERY.

THOMAS MORE (1477–1535), WHO SUCCEEDED CARDINAL WOLSEY AS CHANCELLOR IN 1529, WAS EXECUTED FOR HIGH TREASON.

THOMAS CROMWELL (C.1485–1540), WHO GAINED HENRY VIII'S DIVORCE FROM KATHERINE OF ARAGON AND ORGANIZED THE DISSOLUTION OF THE MONASTERIES (1536–40), WAS EXECUTED FOR TREASON.

I OPPOSED HENRY VIII'S BREAK WITH THE CHURCH OF ROME.

I WAS BLAMED FOR HENRY VIII'S DISASTROUS MARRIAGE TO ANNE OF CLEVES.

EDWARD VI (1537–53), ONLY SON OF HENRY VIII AND JANE SEYMOUR, WAS NINE WHEN HE BECAME KING IN 1547. A REGENCY COUNCIL LED BY HIS UNCLE THE DUKE OF SOMERSET EFFECTIVELY GOVERNED, UNTIL THE DUKE OF NORTHUMBERLAND SEIZED POWER IN 1550, EXECUTED SOMERSET AND BECAME VIRTUAL RULER, BUT WAS HIMSELF EXECUTED BY QUEEN MARY I.

THE DUKE OF NORTHUMBERLAND SUPPORTED A COMPLETE PROTESTANT REFORMATION OF ENGLAND.

QUEEN MARY I (1516–58), KNOWN AS "BLOODY MARY", DAUGHTER OF HENRY VIII AND KATHERINE OF ARAGON, REIGNED FROM 1553 TO 1558 AND MARRIED PHILIP II OF SPAIN.

I TRIED UNSUCCESSFULLY TO RESTORE CATHOLICISM, PERSECUTING ALL PROTESTANT "HERETICS".

THE TUDOR REIGN ENDED WITH ELIZABETH I, AND THE STUART SUCCESSION BEGAN WITH KING JAMES I IN *1603*. THE GLOBE THEATRE, IN WHICH MANY OF SHAKESPEARE'S PLAYS WERE FIRST PRODUCED, BURNED TO GROUND IN *1613*. THE FIRE WAS CAUSED BY SPECIAL GUNPOWDER EFFECTS DURING A PERFORMANCE OF HENRY VIII. SHAKESPEARE RETIRED FROM THE THEATRE A WEALTHY MAN AND RETURNED TO STRATFORD-UPON-AVON.
HE DIED ON ST GEORGE'S DAY, **23** APRIL *1616*.

Following the King's triumphant summit-meeting in France, organized by his ambitious minister Wolsey, there is factional unrest back home at court. Wolsey's arch-rival Buckingham suspects corruption – but Wolsey is a dangerous enemy: after bribing his "Surveyor" to give false evidence, Buckingham is arrested for treason. Praised by the King for thwarting Buckingham's "conspiracy", Wolsey's schemes are opposed by Queen Katherine, who joins Norfolk in condemning him for the savage taxation he has introduced. Of this policy the King knows nothing, and when he orders its cancellation, Wolsey privately seeks the political credit for doing so. The Surveyor testifies that Buckingham intended to murder the King.

Wolsey celebrates by throwing a riotous banquet, which is interrupted by a group of masked revellers – among them the King himself, who is smitten with his dancing-partner: Anne Boleyn by name. Love and politics now begin to interwine. Buckingham forgives his enemies, and dies nobly; Wolsey's schemes continue. Next on his agenda is the divorce between the King and his Catholic Queen, but this is opposed by Norfolk and others, whose appeals to recognize Wolsey's intrigues Henry ignores, instead welcoming Wolsey and the papal legate Campeius, and instructing his unscrupulous secretary Gardiner to initiate formal divorce proceedings. Henry has meanwhile sent an expensive gift to Anne Boleyn...

Despite Katherine's spirited defence against Wolsey, Henry expresses doubts over the sanctity of their marriage (she is the widow of his dead brother Arthur): she is persuaded to accept the divorce to avoid scandal. Wolsey's political success is nevertheless short-lived: he has inadvertently included some incriminating documents in some papers sent to the King, and when Henry returns them, Wolsey realizes the game is up. Arrested and charged by Norfolk, he stoically accepts his fate, advising his deputy, Cromwell, faithfully to serve the King – now newly married to Anne Boleyn. The factionalism continues, though, even on Anne's Coronation Day, this time between Gardiner and Cromwell's friend (and Henry's close adviser) Cranmer.

When word of Wolsey's execution is brought to the ailing Katherine, she forgives him, honouring his Christian repentance after a symbolic dream. From Queen Katherine's death-bed we move to news of Queen Anne's child-bed – she is enduring a dangerous labour. Amidst this uncertainty, King Henry gives Cranmer a signet-ring, symbolic of his royal protection – and then news arrives that Anne has safely given birth to a daughter. When Gardiner accuses Cranmer of heresy in the next day's cabinet-meeting, and orders him to prison, Cranmer reveals the King's ring – whereupon Henry himself emerges to denounce Gardiner's faction, requesting Cranmer to preside over the ceremonial baptism of his new daughter – the future Queen Elizabeth I.

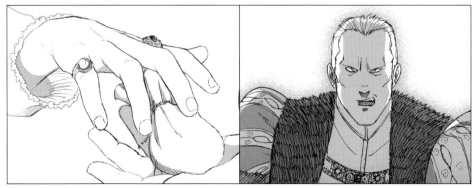

A BRIEF LIFE OF WILLIAM SHAKESPEARE

He learned his craft the hard way. He soon won fame as a playwright with often-staged popular hits.

He and his colleagues formed a stage company, the Lord Chamberlain's Men, which built the famous Globe Theatre. It opened in 1599 but was destroyed by fire in 1613 during a performance of *Henry VIII* which used gunpowder special effects (see p.47). It was rebuilt in brick the following year.

Shakespeare's birthday is traditionally said to be the 23rd of April – St George's Day, patron saint of England. A good start for England's greatest writer. But that date and even his name are uncertain. He signed his own name in different ways. "Shakespeare" is now the accepted one out of dozens of different versions.

He was born at Stratford-upon-Avon in 1564, and baptized on 26th April. His mother, Mary Arden, was the daughter of a prosperous farmer. His father, John Shakespeare, a glove-maker, was a respected civic figure – and probably also a Catholic. In 1570, just as Will began school, his father was accused of illegal dealings. The family fell into debt and disrepute.

Will attended a local school for eight years. He did not go to university. The next ten years are a blank filled by suppositions. Was he briefly a Latin teacher, a soldier, a sea-faring explorer? Was he prosecuted and whipped for poaching deer?

We do know that in 1582 he married Anne Hathaway, eight years his senior, and three months pregnant. Two more children – twins – were born three years later but, by around 1590, Will had left Stratford to pursue a theatre career in London. Shakespeare's apprenticeship began as an actor and "pen for hire".

Shakespeare was a financially successful writer who invested his money wisely in property. In 1597, he bought an enormous house in Stratford, and in 1608 became a shareholder in London's Blackfriars Theatre. He also redeemed the family's honour by acquiring a personal coat of arms.

Shakespeare wrote over 40 works, including poems, "lost" plays and collaborations, in a career spanning nearly 25 years. He retired to Stratford in 1613, where he died on 23rd April 1616, aged 52, apparently of a fever after a "merry meeting" of drinks with friends. Shakespeare did in fact die on St George's Day! He was buried "full 17 foot deep" in Holy Trinity Church, Stratford, and left an epitaph cursing anyone who dared disturb his bones.

There have been preposterous theories disputing Shakespeare's authorship. Some claim that Sir Francis Bacon (1561–1626), philosopher and Lord Chancellor, was the real author of Shakespeare's plays. Others propose Edward de Vere, Earl of Oxford (1550–1604), or, even more weirdly, Queen Elizabeth I. The implication is that the "real" Shakespeare had to be a university graduate or an aristocrat. Nothing less would do for the world's greatest writer.

Shakespeare is mysteriously hidden behind his work. His life will not tell us what inspired his genius.

MANGA SHAKESPEARE ®

EDITORIAL

Richard Appignanesi: Text Adaptor

Richard Appignanesi was a founder and co-director of the Writers & Readers Publishing Cooperative and Icon Books where he originated the internationally acclaimed *Introducing* series. His own best-selling titles in the series include *Freud*, *Postmodernism* and *Existentialism*. He is also the author of the fiction trilogy *Italia Perversa* and the novel *Yukio Mishima's Report to the Emperor*. Currently associate editor of the journal *Third Text* and reviews editor of the journal *Futures*, his latest book *What do Existentialists Believe?* was released in 2006.

Nick de Somogyi: Textual Consultant

Nick de Somogyi works as a freelance writer and researcher, as a genealogist at the College of Arms, and as a contributing editor to *New Theatre Quarterly*. He is the founding editor of the *Globe Quartos* series, and was the visiting curator at Shakespeare's Globe, 2003–6. His publications include *Shakespeare's Theatre of War* (1998), *Jokermen and Thieves: Bob Dylan and the Ballad Tradition* (1986), and (from 2001) the *Shakespeare Folios* series for Nick Hern Books. He has also contributed to the Open University (1995), Carlton Television (2000), and BBC Radio 3 and Radio 4.

ARTIST

Patrick Warren

Patrick Warren graduated with a degree in animation from the University of Westminster. He was a winner of Tokyopop's first UK Rising Stars of Manga competition in 2006. His interest in Japan began when he was eight and he had started doodling manga by the time he was 15. Patrick's influences include manga artists such as Hiroaki Samura, Tite Kubo, Oh! Great and Western artists such as Frank Miller and his own father. *Henry VIII* is Patrick's second full-length manga.

PUBLISHER

SelfMadeHero is a UK-based manga and graphic novel imprint, reinventing some of the most important works of European and world literature. In 2008 SelfMadeHero was named **UK Young Publisher of the Year** at the prestigious British Book Industry Awards.
www.selfmadehero.com

HISTORIC ROYAL PALACES

Historic Royal Palaces is the independent charity that looks after the Tower of London, Hampton Court Palace, the Banqueting House, Kensington Palace and Kew Palace. We help everyone explore the stories of how monarchs and people shaped society, in some of the greatest palaces ever built.
www.hrp.org.uk

SELF MADE HERO

In association with

Historic Royal PALACES